GAME PLAN
FOR LOSS

AN AVERAGE JOE'S GUIDE TO DEALING WITH GRIEF

New York Times Bestselling Author
JOE GIBBS
3-Time Super Bowl Champion and 5-Time NASCAR Champion

TYNDALE
MOMENTUM®

A Tyndale nonfiction imprint

Visit Tyndale online at tyndale.com.

Visit Tyndale Momentum online at tyndalemomentum.com.

Tyndale, Tyndale's quill logo, *Tyndale Momentum*, and the Tyndale Momentum logo are registered trademarks of Tyndale House Ministries. Tyndale Momentum is the nonfiction imprint of Tyndale House Publishers, Carol Stream, Illinois.

Game Plan for Loss: An Average Joe's Guide to Dealing with Grief

Designed by Ron C. Kaufmann

For information about special discounts for bulk purchases, please contact Tyndale House Publishers at csresponse@tyndale.com, or call 1-855-277-9400.

Library of Congress Cataloging-in-Publication Data

A catalog record for this book is available from the Library of Congress.

ISBN 978-1-4964-5795-0

Printed in China

28	27	26	25	24	23	22
7	6	5	4	3	2	1

CONTENTS

A Note from the Coach *vii*

A Note from the Coach

I'VE GIVEN A LOT OF speeches in my life, but none was as important or as difficult as the one I had to make on January 25, 2019. I had been asked by my daughter-in-law, Melissa, to give the opening prayer at the memorial service for her husband—and my son—J.D.

J.D.'s fight with a rare degenerative brain disease took place over the span of five years, during which, little by little, he lost everything—first his spark, then his speech, then his movement, and eventually his life. We tried everything to help J.D.—doctors, specialists, consortiums, experimental trials, faith-based healing services, physical rehab—*everything*. But on January 11, 2019, the Lord chose to take J.D. home.

Those five years were the longest and hardest of my entire life. I'd been through difficult times before. I've had financial disasters, professional crises, and even a few health issues of my own, but watching J.D. slowly slip away and not being able to do anything to stop it was the most helpless feeling in the world.

I have spent my entire professional life geared to win, not lose. During my tenure in the NFL, I was fortunate enough to coach the Washington Redskins to three Super Bowl victories, and as a race team owner, our teams have won five NASCAR Cup Series championships. Between football and racing, I have spent more than fifty years trying to figure out how to win. I can't tell you how many late nights I spent crafting game plans against the Cowboys, the Eagles, and the Giants, trying to account for every possible situation.

The same goes for racing. I realize it may look like we're just driving around in circles out there, but believe me, there is *a lot* of planning that goes into race day—from calculating fuel mileage to figuring out how many more laps you can get on a given set of tires. Even the temperature and the amount of rubber on the track as the race goes on gets taken into consideration.

The point is, whether you're working between

the hash marks or along the oval, if you want to win, you've got to plan for every possible scenario, be prepared for anything, and leave nothing—and I mean *nothing*—to chance.

The same goes for life. As a Christian, I believe God gave us the ultimate game plan for success in the Bible, so a little over a decade ago, I brought together a team of top scholars and theologians to help me write what I called *Game Plan for Life*. In it, we addressed eleven areas that I believe *all* of us need to have a game plan for in order to win at the game of life, because at the end of the day, that's the biggest game of all.

So why am I writing a book about loss? Well, here's the thing. When J.D. got sick and went to be with the Lord, I did not have a game plan for what I went through. In fact, all the scholars and theologians in the world could not have prepared me for what I was about to face. Frankly, I'm not sure *anything* can prepare you for the pain of watching a loved one slowly slip away. And when the wreckage of those five horrible years finally cleared, I found myself struggling with a lot of questions. Five, to be exact.

Why didn't God show up? Whenever I had faced difficult circumstances before, I always felt as though God was right there beside me, walking through my struggle with me. But during the whole of J.D.'s illness, God just did not seem to be there. I tried. I prayed. I literally begged. But I just couldn't see that he was there.

Are we just living a life of chance? I have always believed that God holds all the power, but J.D.'s illness made me wonder, does God allow bad things to enter our lives for a reason, or do bad things just randomly happen to us?

Why do Christians suffer? I know I'm biased, but J.D. was one of the godliest young men you could ever hope to meet. From the time he could walk and toddle, he always tried to be the right kind of person. Truth be told, he was the real spiritual leader of our family. So why did *he* have to suffer the way he did?

Why do some Christians suffer more than others? J.D.'s battle was not quick, and it was not easy. His wife, Melissa, their four boys, our son Coy and his family, and my wife, Pat, and I watched him slowly slip away over the course of five incredibly long, painful years. It was hard enough losing J.D. as it was. Why didn't the Lord just take him quickly and spare his family and friends the pain of watching him suffer for so long?

And finally, *Do we really reap what we sow?* The Bible assures us that we do and that "in all things God works for the good of those who love him, who have been called according to his purpose" (Romans 8:28). And as I said before, J.D. lived a godly, Christ-centered life, but no matter how hard I tried, I could not see the good in his leaving us the way he did.

Now, none of these issues caused me to question my salvation or my faith in the Lord. I know He created me and that I belong to Him. But as I stood there waiting to walk onto that stage and lead an auditorium full of J.D.'s family and friends in prayer, all of these questions came at me at once. And if *I* was struggling with them, I figured there was a good chance a lot of other people were struggling with them as well.

This book is my attempt to answer these five questions. And while I did consult with several pastors along the way, the revelations and ideas you are about to read are *my* answers to these five questions. I'm not a scholar or a theologian. In fact, I'm about as far away from being an intellectual as you can get. I'm just your average

Joe—a dad trying to come to grips with the loss of his son. I hope some of what I've learned can help you. I know it may not feel like it at the moment, but I promise you, God *is* there, He *is* listening, He *does* have a plan, and He *does* work all things together for good for those who love and serve Him. Believe me. I've experienced it.

Joe Gibbs

1
"I'M TRYIN'!"

AS I WATCHED THE MASS of sweaty bodies pushing, shoving, and knocking each other around in a big, disorganized scrum, one word came to mind—*mayhem*. I'd seen plenty of skirmishes out on the football field, but nothing compared to the chaos playing out in front of me that day.

It was Saturday morning, and my wife, Pat, and I were at the local elementary school watching a bunch of five-year-olds armed with wooden hockey sticks chasing a little orange puck around the gymnasium floor. And smackdab in the middle of that mob was our son J.D. It was his first organized sport, and like most dads,

I was locked onto J.D. like a laser. And that kid was hustling. I mean, wherever that little puck went, J.D. was right there after it, fighting and scrapping his heart out.

Eventually that mass of kids made its way over to the stands just below where Pat and I were sitting. I put my hands up to my mouth, and as loud as I could, I yelled, "J.D., get it!" That kid stopped right in his tracks, looked up at me, his face bright red, and hollered back every bit as loud, "I'm tryin'!"

Right then and there I knew there was no point in ever yelling at J.D., because no matter what that kid was doing, he was always trying his hardest.

Making an Impact

Before we get to my five questions, let me tell you a little about J.D. so you can see where I'm coming from.

J.D. never did anything halfway. From the moment he gave his life to Christ at age six, it was obvious to Pat and me that he was determined to become the best person he could be. Other kids were just naturally drawn to him—in part because he was drawn to them. J.D. liked everybody. He didn't care about social circles, who was popular and who wasn't. He wanted everyone to feel special. In fact, he used to make a point of seeking out the less popular kids at school to try and make a connection. And let me tell you, when the varsity quarterback sits down at a cafeteria table full of kids he doesn't know and says, "Hi, my name's J.D. How are you guys doing today?" it makes an impact.

Pat and I used to host Young Life get-togethers over at the house when J.D. was in high school, and I can't tell you how many kids, many who had no interest in faith whatsoever, would show up week in and week out at J.D.'s invitation. J.D. didn't drink or smoke or cuss. He was just a fun, outgoing, friendly guy who loved the Lord and genuinely cared about people. A lot of those kids even gave their own lives to Christ as a result of those get-togethers, including both of J.D.'s best friends, Moose Valliere and Dave Alpern (who is now the president of Joe Gibbs Racing). And do you know what? I have no doubt those commitments meant more to J.D. than any football game he ever played in.

When it came time to go to college, J.D. was offered a scholarship to play football at William and Mary. That's where he and Melissa started dating seriously. They had been middle school sweethearts, but her family moved to South Carolina right around the time they started high school. Then she came out to Williamsburg for a visit during J.D.'s sophomore year, and the sparks started flying again. Shortly after he graduated from William and Mary, J.D. proposed and she said yes. Now, I've said this before with regard to Pat, but sometimes God just gives you the perfect wife. Well, God could not have given J.D. a more perfect wife than Melissa. You'll understand why soon enough.

My point is, as I said, J.D. never did anything halfway. And though much of this book will focus on him, I can tell you my other son, Coy, is the exact same way.

Coy was five foot eleven, 220 pounds in high school, and he played middle linebacker. His senior year, he was recruited by Stanford, and I told him, "Hey, look, if you go to Stanford, you're going to have to red shirt. You're probably going to have to play special teams before you ever get to play a snap on defense." But typical Coy, he went out there, started the second game of his freshman year, and never came back out. He played four straight years at middle linebacker. His senior year, the team picked him to do the speech at the closing banquet. They told him he could talk about whatever he wanted. Well, Coy talked about all the kids on the team that showed up for practice every day and worked their tails off but never got a chance to play. That's just the kind of guy he is.

I'm telling you, Pat and I were blessed with two amazing sons.

"Hey, Dad. Let's Start a Race Team."

Growing up, both of our boys loved all things motorized—Jet Skis, go-karts, motorbikes. If it had an engine and went fast, J.D. and Coy were all over it. Truth be told, they probably got that from me. As a kid, I was more of a football, basketball, and baseball fan, but when I was sixteen, we moved to California, and back then, Southern California was all about hot rods and drag racing. That's when I fell in love with and started working on cars. They weren't expensive hot rods, which was probably a blessing, because I had no idea what I was doing. In fact, Pat and I used to joke that we got towed out of every drive-in in Southern California because once I got through working on a car, it was never the same again.

Anyway, I used to take J.D. and Coy to the races, and before long, they both developed an interest in all kinds of racing. Then right about the time J.D. was set to graduate, he and Coy started prompting me to start a race team.

Now, you could have fit what I knew about starting a NASCAR team into a thimble, but one of my biggest regrets is how much of my boys' lives I missed because of football, and I figured starting a race team would give us an opportunity to spend more time together. So I made a few calls, somehow managed to convince Norm Miller at Interstate Batteries that I was a good risk for sponsorship, and in 1991, while Coy was off playing football at Stanford, my good friend Don Meredith (not the football player), Todd Meredith (Don's son), Dave Alpern, Jimmy Makar, J.D., and I started Joe Gibbs Racing. Don and I had started several ministries together, and he was instrumental in helping us get Joe Gibbs Racing (JGR) off the ground.

J.D. started out working in the pits as a tire changer, but before long, his people skills, steady demeanor, and sharp business mindset made him a natural fit to take over as president of JGR.

J.D.'s passion for the race team was unparalleled, and he never shied away from voicing his opinions. In fact, he and Dave used to get into scraps all the time about everything from drivers' contracts to marketing budgets, but true to his nature, J.D. was always diplomatic, he never took things personally, and he never held a grudge. And he *always* cared about our people and thought of them as family.

I remember back when we stopped building our race team motors and had to lay off ten people in our motor room. Unbeknownst to all of us, J.D. had set aside some money for those guys—a *lot* of money, actually—and then he followed each one of them through their transition process. He had a huge heart for people and felt very strongly that everyone should be treated fairly.

From time to time, questions would come up like, *Should we try to hire somebody from another team?* Well, there's a right way of doing that and a wrong way. J.D. was always adamant that things be done the right way, and he held everyone else to that standard as well. In fact,

it's because of J.D. that we have several chaplains on staff at JGR and Bible studies every
Wednesday. J.D. also instituted a giving ministry at JGR that currently supports more than
fifty different ministries around the world. Let's
just say, if something good was happening at
JGR, odds were, J.D. was behind it.

As the race team continued to grow, so did
J.D.'s family. He and Melissa had four sons—
Jackson, Miller, Jason, and Taylor—and just like
everything else in his life, J.D. was committed
to being the best dad he could be. He and the
boys were always off somewhere hiking, skiing,
mountain biking, or playing football, basketball,
or baseball. And as dedicated as he was to the
race team, he never let work get in the way of
spending time with his boys. We could be smackdab in the middle of a crisis, and J.D. would look
at his watch and say, "Well . . . if it's not this, it's
going to be something else." Then he'd just walk
out the door. Later that day, I might ride by his
house and see a full-blown football game going
on in the backyard.

Of course, as I already mentioned, J.D. was
passionate about Young Life, and that continued
beyond his teen years. He and Melissa would

take the whole family to Young Life Family Camp every summer. He even served on their national board of directors.

His entire life, whatever J.D. did, he did 100 percent. That's why, in the summer of 2014, we all knew something was wrong.

A Sudden Shift

Midway through our 2014 season, we started noticing changes with J.D. He became quieter in meetings, less engaged. Instead of taking part in the discussions, he would just sit there quietly. And instead of making the rounds through the shop every day, visiting with and checking in on employees, he would sit in his office for hours working on his computer. I figured he was going through some kind of midlife crisis, that maybe he had just grown tired of racing and wanted to do something else. I mean, running a racing team is a *lot* of work, and J.D. had been going at it full tilt for twenty-three years. But whenever I asked him if anything was bothering him, he'd just say, "No, I'm fine." Then on August 19, we held a press conference to announce that Carl Edwards would be joining JGR in the 2015 season to drive our new #19 car. J.D. was normally a bundle of energy at media events, speaking off the cuff, working the crowd, and joking with the press. So when he got up there and had difficulty with his speech, I *knew* something was wrong.

The next day, while J.D. was at work, I went over to his house to talk to Melissa. "Listen," I said to her. "Something's off with J.D. He's been a lot quieter lately, withdrawn. He just seems disinterested with everything that's going on at work, and I'm wondering if maybe he's going through some kind of midlife crisis." As soon as I said that, Melissa looked up at me. Realizing what I'd just implied, I quickly added, "I mean, I know J.D. loves ministry work and that you two have talked about going into it full-time some-day, and if that's what he wants to do, that's . . ."

"I know what you're talking about," she said, cutting me off midsentence. "I've noticed it, too." Then she paused for a second. "I think it could be something physical."

I had never even considered that. But once Melissa told me that J.D. had been acting differently around the house for the past several months as well—not spending as much time playing with the boys, keeping to himself, and obsessing over simple chores like doing the dishes or folding laundry—I started to think she might be right.

Looking for Answers

Two days later, J.D., Melissa, Pat, and I flew out to the Mayo Clinic in Rochester, Minnesota, to see if we could find some answers. Over the course of the next two days, they ran every test you could think of on J.D.: CAT scans, PET scans, MRIs, blood work, verbal tests, cognitive tests, neuropsychological tests—the whole nine yards. I was optimistic. I told Pat, "Once we know what we're dealing with, we can fix it."

Unfortunately, the diagnosis wasn't quite what we were expecting. In fact, it wasn't really a diagnosis at all. After two solid days of testing, all the doctors could tell us was, "We're not really sure what it is." They suspected it was some kind of degenerative brain disease—possibly early onset Alzheimer's—but they couldn't say for certain. All they could say is that he would likely decline over time. When we asked about next steps, they just said, "Get lots of sleep, eat a healthy diet—and prove us wrong."

I was devastated. I mean that's not what you want to hear from a doctor. Here I was, asking,

"How do we fix this?" and basically, what they were saying was, there is no fix. And this was Mayo. These were supposed to be the best medical people in the world. I don't think I've ever felt so discouraged.

And so, we went back home, and for the first few weeks, we were resigned to the fact that there was nothing we could do but wait and pray for healing. But as J.D.'s condition continued to worsen, the fighter in me took over. If the doctors weren't going to find a way to help J.D., we would.

A friend of Melissa's made us aware of the Tau Consortium in San Francisco. Tau is a protein inside the brain, and when it becomes "tangled," so to speak, you end up with things like chronic traumatic encephalopathy (CTE), Alzheimer's, dementia, and other neurodegenerative disorders. The Tau Consortium consists of over thirty doctors, all of whom are doing research exclusively on tau, and we figured, if anyone would be able to help J.D., it would be them. So J.D. and I made the trip out to meet with them.

By this point, J.D. was starting to have trouble with his motor skills and needed a little help dressing and undressing, so we got adjoining rooms at the hotel. The morning after we arrived, I went over to J.D.'s room to get him, and he wasn't there. I panicked. I immediately went down to the lobby, and there he was, sitting at a little table, trying to write a happy birthday card to his youngest son, Taylor. Now, J.D. always had horrible handwriting, but to see him struggling the way he was, trying to fight through it . . . it just broke my heart. My mind flashed back to that scrappy five-year-old chasing that hockey puck around the gymnasium floor, and it was all I could do to keep from crying. God bless that boy. As always, he was *tryin'.*

The Trial

When we met with the team at the Consortium, we learned that two scientists there had developed an antibody that they hoped might be a cure for tau-related diseases and that a big pharmaceutical company had purchased the antibody and was getting ready to start a clinical trial.

When I heard that, it was like an answer to prayer. I thought, *Maybe this is the reason J.D. got sick.* Maybe God was using J.D.'s illness as a way to say to everybody in the world, "Hey, there's something here that could really help people."

Surely God was going to use this trial to cure J.D. All we had to do was get him into it.

But when we appealed to the pharmaceutical company running the trial, they told us J.D. could only enter under a "compassionate use waiver." In other words, we had to prove that this antibody was his only hope for survival. I tell you, I've never been more upset. When the best doctors in the world tell you there's no hope, and then you find out there's a possible cure, only to be told you may not qualify . . . talk about being disappointed.

I went to every high-profile person I knew who might carry some influence and asked them to intervene on J.D.'s behalf. I also had all his medical records sent over, as well as all the test results and the prognosis from Mayo. Getting J.D. into that trial became the most important thing in my life.

Finally, one day, the phone rang. It was the CEO of the pharmaceutical company running the trial. He said, "Joe, you have got to stop this. I promise you, we'll look at J.D.'s. records, make the appropriate decision, and admit him if he qualifies, but you have got to back off." Well, that got through to me. I backed off and just prayed with all my heart that J.D.'s medical history would be enough to get him in.

Two weeks later, a doctor with the Tau Consortium called. J.D. had been admitted to the trial. It was one of the most emotional days of my life. We had all been praying so hard for healing. Surely, this was the answer we'd been waiting for.

The trial took place at the University of North Carolina at Chapel Hill. Once a month, either Melissa or I would take J.D. over there, and he would receive the antibody intravenously. Because this had never been tried before, we had no idea what to expect. So while we waited for the antibody to do its work, we began an aggressive approach of our own between infusions.

Melissa arranged for a team of caregivers to come out to JGR every day and work with J.D. We had both a speech and a physical therapist, as well as a personal trainer, each of whom would work with J.D., and then we would go out for long walks with him in the afternoon. Meanwhile, Melissa was consumed with researching neurological diseases and monitoring J.D.'s progress. If that disease was going to take J.D., it was going to have to go through us first. And we were going to fight it every step of the way.

We were twelve months into the trial when J.D.'s physician said to us, "I think we need to end the program. I'm sorry, but as far as we can tell, nothing is happening with J.D."

We asked him if he would please give it a few more months. Pat and I had both been praying like crazy for a miracle, and I was convinced this antibody was it. We just needed to give it more time. He agreed to give it two more months, but when the final two infusions failed to make a difference, J.D. was officially dropped from the trial. I was devastated. I thought for sure God was going to heal J.D. But not only had the antibody failed to work, in spite of all the therapy we had been doing, J.D.'s condition had continued to decline.

Waiting on God

We still firmly believed God could and would heal J.D., so Melissa began researching different Christian healing ministries. There were several she had heard about, and there were a lot of people claiming they worked. We went to several churches, to revivals in the Carolinas, and

even to a California church known for heal-
ings. They were very intense, emotional events.
Pastors and congregants would lay hands on
J.D. and pray over him. They would say things
like "He's healed." Or "It may take a while for the
healing to manifest." Others would say, "I can
feel the power coming through J.D." As much as
we prayed for those words to be true, week after
week passed, and there was no healing.

When the healing services failed to bring
about any results, I became even more adamant about increasing J.D.'s therapy sessions.
But one day, J.D.'s doctor pulled me aside and
said, "Look, J.D. wouldn't want this. You're fighting every inch of the way to keep him going, and
I understand why you're doing it, but it's not
what's best for J.D. right now, and it's not good
for you, either."

I came to find out it was Melissa who
prompted the doctor to talk with me. Melissa
and I had differing ideas on how to proceed. I
wanted to increase the therapy, but Melissa
knew where we were headed, and her approach
was to have J.D. at home, with his therapy more
family centered. She loved J.D. dearly, but she
was also able to see what I couldn't—that this

disease was taking J.D. to a point of no return. And all the time I was spending on therapy and last-ditch efforts to bring him back was making it harder on J.D., Melissa, and the family. There were several times when Mel had to sit me down and remind me that she was and should be J.D.'s main caregiver.

"Look," she said to me, "I know where this is going. I just want J.D. to be comfortable and to take care of him as best we can with what time we have left." Melissa took her role as a caregiver very seriously, and there was never any question that taking care of J.D. was her number-one priority. While we may have disagreed about what that should look like, her unconditional love for J.D. and the way she took care of both him and those boys was incredible.

She wanted their lives to continue. She didn't want J.D.'s illness to take away any more from those boys than it already had. And J.D. wouldn't have wanted that either. So she made a deliberate point of keeping their lives as normal as possible. Even when J.D. was no longer able to walk or communicate, she always included him in every family outing and activity. And because Melissa set the standard, the boys adapted to an otherwise impossible situation. They openly accepted their dad's condition, and they were never once embarrassed by it. They would still have friends over to use the pool, eat dinner, and spend the night. Heck, Miller always had at least two or three guys hanging around the house.

Thanks to Melissa, they somehow had the ability to say, "This is our life. This is what we do." And whenever Melissa called on them to help with J.D., they were all in. They never grumbled, never complained. They just did whatever their mom—and dad—needed them to do. Words cannot express how grateful Pat and I were for that.

Saying Goodbye

We spent the next two and a half years watching J.D. slowly slip away from us. Little by little, he lost more and more. To watch someone you love fade away day by day . . . there really aren't words. J.D. had always been so full of life, and what this disease did to him was horrible. I kept praying, *God, if you're going to take J.D., please take him now. Don't let him continue to suffer like this. Don't make his family—his boys—go through this.*

I arranged my schedule at JGR so I could spend as much time as possible with him. Though he was unable to communicate, I enjoyed just sitting with him. Honestly, I felt like I loved him more when he was sick than I did when he was healthy. It's hard to even put it into words. I respected him so much—the way he lived his life. I just wanted to be with him, to hold him, to hug him, and to love him.

During the final weeks of J.D.'s life, I finally accepted that he was not going to win his battle. Still, I could not understand why God didn't intervene. Why He was letting J.D. go through such a long and difficult struggle. Or why J.D. had to go through it at all. Pat and I spent many nights sitting up late talking, praying, and crying. Honestly, going through those last days . . . nothing could have been more painful.

Melissa, Jackson, Miller, Jason, Taylor, Pat, and I were all there when J.D. went to be with the Lord on January 11, 2019.

Melissa immediately set to work planning the service to honor J.D.'s life. The service took place a little over two weeks later at John M. Belk Arena at Davidson College. Dave Alpern joked in his eulogy that it seemed fitting that J.D.'s memorial would take place in a gym. Honestly, it was probably the only place big enough to hold all the people J.D. had impacted during his forty-nine short years here on Earth. Melissa was adamant that the service not be a time of weeping but a celebration of life that would honor the Lord, and hopefully, lead others to Christ as a result. After all, that's what J.D. would have wanted.

The service featured godly music, testimonials, and eulogies by his friends and his brother, Coy. Jackson, Miller, Jason, and Taylor all read excerpts from J.D.'s daily journals, and I was charged with opening the service in prayer.

I started by thanking Melissa for taking such wonderful and loving care of J.D., and then I thanked God for letting us enjoy J.D. for forty-nine years. I thanked Him for making J.D. a little boy who loved life and for making him a godly father, husband, and friend with a caring heart, who was always helping others in need. I thanked Him for giving J.D. the right priorities in life—God first, then his family, and then others. And I told Him how excited I was that J.D. would continue to influence others through his boys and all the other people whose lives he touched, and I said how much I looked forward to someday spending eternity with J.D. in heaven. I closed with one final request—that God let J.D. know how much we all looked up to him and missed him and to please take care of him until we come home.

We made a point of directing everyone to a special website we set up in J.D.'s name, jdgibbslegacy.com, and we invited anyone with questions about dedicating their lives to Christ to reach out to us via e-mail, letter, text, or phone. We also posted the full memorial service online, and to date more than nine million people have viewed that service. In the days and weeks that followed, we received hundreds of e-mails and letters from people telling us what an enormous impact J.D. had on them. A lot of men wrote to tell me that listening to J.D.'s boys read from his daily journals inspired them to spend more time with their families. Many even commented that they planned to start their own daily logs so their kids would have something to remember them by. Honestly, the response was a little overwhelming.

I'm Tryin'

As wonderful as it was to see the impact J.D. was continuing to have on others, I was still struggling. For five years, I had dedicated myself to fighting this horrible disease to the point that it became my whole life. Now that it was over, as I mentioned at the start of this book, I was left with so many questions.

Why didn't God show up? Every other time I'd faced adversity in my life, God had always shown up. And yet for five long years, I prayed continually for God to intervene, and He never did.

Why J.D.? Why would a godly guy like J.D. be forced to endure such long and horrible suffering? I know people would probably say, "You're his dad; you saw him through rose-colored glasses," but I'm telling you, you can talk to anybody who knew J.D., and they would tell you the same. So why did this happen to *him*?

And why didn't God just take J.D. home quickly? Why make him go through such a long journey?

Before J.D.'s illness, I'd always had a confidence that if I lived a godly life, then God was going to be there for me. All my life, I've heard preachers say that we reap what we sow and that everything works out for those who love the Lord. J.D. loved the Lord and lived a godly life, but did

J.D. really reap what he sowed? Did things work out the best for him in the end?

I mean, if something like this could happen to someone like J.D., what about my grandkids? I had always believed that God was in control of everything, but now I had questions. Is it possible that our lives here on earth are lived solely by chance?

As much as I tried, I couldn't reconcile what I'd just been through with what I'd always believed as a Christian. Those questions just kept circling around in my mind. J.D.'s journey may have ended, but mine had just begun.

I spent the next several months studying the Bible, praying for clarity, and meeting with different pastors, trying to find answers to these questions. Again, I'm not a theologian or biblical scholar. I'm just a dad trying to come to grips with the loss of his son. But if what I've learned can be of any help to you as you work through your own grieving process, my journey, difficult as it has been, will have been worth it.

2

"WHY DIDN'T GOD SHOW UP?"

DO YOU BELIEVE IN ANGELS? Well, I sure do, and here's why.[1]

In the early days of my career, I wanted to be a head coach so badly, I could taste it. My dream was to be a head coach in the NFL, but I applied for top college jobs too. After spending four seasons under Don Coryell at St. Louis as the running backs coach, I thought that moving on to the Tampa Bay Buccaneers for the 1978 season to be John McKay's offensive coordinator was just the right move. But John was used to calling his own plays. By the end of the year, he had reinserted himself as the one calling the plays, and the season became a nightmare for me. I was frustrated, and we had an awful year. After having told myself at the beginning of the season, "This is it, God's plan, what He has been preparing me for," I had hit a new low. I couldn't hold my hand out in front of me without it shaking like a leaf. Here I was in my late thirties, and I thought my dream was gone. No one would want to make a head coach out of an offensive coordinator whose team wasn't a winner.

At the end of the season, I agonized over whether to stay in Tampa or try to find another team. Meanwhile, Don Coryell had left the Cardinals and had been hired as head coach of the San Diego Chargers. When I heard that, I prayed, "Lord, don't have him call me unless You want me to leave Tampa Bay."

Sure enough, the next morning, Coryell called. But he wasn't offering the offensive coordinator's job. If I went to San Diego, I would be an assistant coach again, a demotion. I was torn. I loved coaching under Coryell, but I wanted to stay on track for a head coaching job. But if I stayed in Tampa as the offensive coordinator, there was no guarantee things would work out any better.

While I was waiting for my turn to talk with

Coach McKay about the future, three assistants of his who had been with him forever came out of their postseason meetings with him only to report they had been let go. I got a sinking feeling. Maybe this was my time to get fired too. At least I had the offer from Coryell. I wouldn't be out of work, but I'd sure be taking a step back. And though it happens a lot, no coach wants a firing on his résumé.

When I finally got into John's office, he said, "Hey, I want you to stay." He added that he wanted to keep calling the plays, but said, "I want you here."

I told him I'd think about it, and we agreed to meet the next morning. And boy, did I think about it! I couldn't think of anything else. Should I stay in a bad situation and hope it turned around so I'd look like an offensive coordinator worth taking a chance on as a head coach? Or should I take the demotion and work for Don Coryell again, hoping for a break? I talked it over with Pat, wrote out all the pros and cons, prayed over it, and stayed up all night.

In the morning, while I was getting ready to go, I told Pat, "I still have no idea what to do."

She suggested I go to the meeting with no agenda. "Just let him do the talking. You say nothing until you're ready."

Pat really does have great wisdom! On the drive in, I resolved to wait—in absolute silence, if necessary, even if it went on for fifteen minutes. I wouldn't say a thing, not one word, until I had heard John out and had a real solid feeling about how I should respond.

When I got to the meeting, Coach McKay had a yellow pad in front of him, and he went down a long list of things he wanted to talk about, reiterating that he wanted to call the plays but that he wanted me to stay, and on and on. The longer he talked, the more certain I became that it was time for me to move on.

I told him his ideas were good and sound and that I appreciated the opportunity he'd given me and added, "But I've made up my mind, and I want to leave."

John was great about it. Though he tried to talk me into staying, we parted as friends. I believed I had made the right decision, but I was still in turmoil. Should I go with Coryell to San Diego, taking the demotion? I couldn't relax, couldn't sit still. My mind was all over the place, and the more I talked with Pat about it, the more restless I became. I decided I needed to talk to my spiritual father, George Tharel.

I flew into Fort Smith, Arkansas, to connect to a flight to Fayetteville; but when I got to Fort Smith, it was snowing hard, and the next flight was canceled. I pleaded with God to let me get to Fayetteville, knowing I was doing the right thing in trying to see George. Then I overheard a couple of guys talking about renting a car.

I said, "You going to Fayetteville?"

They looked at me warily. "Yeah."

"I'm going with you."

No suggesting, no asking, I just announced it and climbed into the back seat of their rental.

It quickly became clear they had never driven in snow before. We took off down the freeway, and within a mile and a half I could tell we'd never make it. It was hilly and slippery, and the car was all over the road.

Well, these guys thought I was crazy anyway, so when I insisted they pull over, they were more than happy to let me out. Now I was on the wrong side of the highway and had to lug my bags over the median. My glasses were all fogged up, I was freezing, and worst of all, I felt defeated.

What was going on? All I was trying to do was get to my spiritual father, and God wasn't going to let me do that? I hitched a ride back to the airport and checked in for a flight back to Tampa. As I sat down to wait and thaw out a little, what did I notice on a table right near where I was sitting? A Bible. Strange.

Curious, I flipped it open to the first chapter of James, which I'd been studying recently because it deals with making decisions. All of a sudden, I felt a nudge on my shoulder, and a guy said, "I claimed that chapter in my life about six months ago."

What? I couldn't believe it. With everything that had already happened that day, I found a Bible where one shouldn't be, and I turned to a specific passage—and then a stranger comes along and says he recently claimed that very same passage for himself? This was too bizarre. All I could manage was, "Really?" and then he told me his story.

He was a pharmacist, and he had moved to his dream job in another state only to discover that he had to pass a huge pharmaceutical test once he arrived. He had been out of school for a long time, and there was no way he'd be able to pass such a test.

He told me he had been in a real quandary, wondering why he had left his home state and a good job, chasing a dream, only to see it come crashing down. He said he had studied that first chapter of James and finally came to the end of himself. "I told the Lord, 'I'm done. I'm turning this all over to You. You know what I want to do in life, but I can't do this. I'm going to have to trust You.' And would you believe it? I went in and breezed that hard test, and now I'm loving the best job in the world."

I was speechless. Some would call this a co-incidence, but I knew better. I hardly had time to even respond. My plane was boarding, and I never saw that guy again. But one thing I know for sure: Whether he was an angel or just someone I needed to run into right then, God put him there specifically for me. I got back on that plane and told God, "I get it. I am going to quit worrying about being a head coach. If it happens, it happens. I am trusting you, God, with my coaching career." And from that day forward, I did.

Simply put, when I needed help, God showed up.

Is Anybody There?

All my life, whenever I had faced a difficult decision or situation, God had always shown up. And then J.D. got sick. For five years, I prayed for God to intervene. I prayed that the doctors at Mayo would be able to help him. I prayed that the tau antibody would help him. I prayed that the healing ministries we participated in would help him. I prayed that the speech and physical therapists we brought in would help him. But not once during those five long, horrible years did I ever see God show up. It was as though He just went quiet.

Or did He?

There is a section in Matthew right after the Crucifixion where the newly resurrected Christ calls His disciples together and tells them to "go and make disciples of all nations, baptizing them in the name of the Father and of the Son and of the Holy Spirit, and teaching them to obey everything I have commanded you." Then He says, "And surely I am with you always, to the very end of the age" (Matthew 28:19-20).

Surely I am with you always, to the very end of the age.

Now I've said before that J.D.'s illness never made me question my faith in the Lord, and it didn't. I want to make that perfectly clear. But when all my prayers for healing went unanswered, it really shook me. It felt like God had abandoned me when I needed Him most. Yet the Bible promises us that God will always be with us. And the Bible isn't just a book; it's a direct message from God to us. So when Jesus says, "Surely I am with you always," you can believe it—even if you can't always see it.

So if God didn't show up as I expected Him to, how *did* God show up in J.D.'s illness and death?

He Showed Up

On February 16, 2019, a little over a month after J.D. went to be with the Lord, the NASCAR season kicked off with the biggest race of the year, the Daytona 500.

A few weeks before the race, Denny Hamlin, who drives our #11 FedEx car, came to us with a special request. All our drivers have their names printed right above the door of their cars. Denny wanted to know if he could put J.D.'s name next to his.

You see, Denny and J.D. had a special relationship. J.D. was the one who found Denny back when he was racing late models in Manassas, Virginia. Denny's parents had sacrificed everything to help him get into racing, and they were just about to give up when J.D. came along and offered Denny an opportunity to participate in a manufacturer's test drive. Denny absolutely killed it in that test drive, so J.D. put Denny in one of our Xfinity cars at Darlington, which is one of our hardest tracks—even veteran drivers will attest to that— and Denny finished in eighth place. J.D. looked at me and said, "Dad, I think we need to sign this guy." And I agreed. So when Denny asked if he could add J.D.'s name next to his over the door, we said, "Definitely."

As it happens, NASCAR had also reached out to us and said that they wanted to honor J.D. during one of the laps. That sounded great to me—J.D. would have loved that. When they asked which lap I wanted, I didn't even have to think about it. "Let's do 11."

J.D. had worn #11 on his jersey all through high school. Plus, Denny would be driving the #11 car with J.D.'s name over the door, and J.D. had gone home to be with the Lord on January 11, so it just felt right.

I've already mentioned that the Daytona 500 is our biggest race. It's kind of NASCAR's equivalent to the Super Bowl. The fact that it comes first makes absolutely no sense, but that's NASCAR. It's also one of the hardest races to win, and the season before had been Denny's worst year since joining the team. He didn't win a single race.

So the odds against him winning the 500 were astronomical. When the eleventh lap started, everyone stood up along the pit wall, and the announcers talked about J.D. as the camera followed Denny's car around the track. Our whole family was there. It was extremely emotional and a really wonderful moment.

The race continued, and like I said, the 500 is one of the most difficult races to win. For one thing, it's a restrictor plate race. I won't get into all the engineering behind it. Suffice it to say, it basically means that the cars usually end up circling the track in a tightly formed pack. And when cars travel in packs around an oval at high speeds, all it takes is one car to make a wrong move, and next thing you know, there's a huge wreck. In racing they call it "the big one." Well, true to form, there were several "big ones" during this race, and yet somehow, three of our drivers—Kyle Busch, Erik Jones, and Denny—made it through all of them. And when the white flag came out signaling the final lap, all three of them were right up front. And wouldn't you know, Denny won! Not only that, Kyle came in second, and Erik came in third. JGR had pulled off the hat trick. It was only the second time in the history of the 500 that that had ever happened.

As you can imagine, our whole team was in tears. It had been such an emotional year. Actually, it had been an emotional *five* years. But standing there in that winner's circle, watching Denny surrounded by television cameras, talking to the media, telling them about J.D. and pointing to J.D.'s name above the door of his car, it suddenly hit me that nearly ten million people were watching this race. That meant ten million people were hearing J.D.'s story. Ten million people were hearing J.D.'s testimony. *Ten million people.*

God had shown up.

In the days following that race, we had letters and e-mails come in from people all over the country telling us that the race was one of the most emotional things they'd ever seen and that surely God had orchestrated all of it on J.D.'s behalf. And we referred everyone who reached out to us to the legacy page we'd set up for J.D., where they could watch J.D.'s memorial service, read his story, and hear about his love for the Lord. As I mentioned earlier, as of the writing of this book, more than nine million people, via the website or social media, have watched that service, many of whom have written to tell us they have accepted the Lord as their Savior. Talk about making an impact! As I said, J.D. never did anything halfway.

The Rearview Mirror

After the dust had settled on the 2019 season and I had time to reflect on everything that had happened, I realized that the 500 wasn't the only time God had shown up.

One time, I had taken J.D. and the boys out to a restaurant that we all loved just down the road from JGR. J.D.'s illness had progressed to the point where he was having a hard time swallowing. Well, we were all eating, and the boys and I were laughing and talking away at the table, and I guess I must not have been paying close enough attention to J.D., because all of a sudden, he started choking, and before I knew it, he stopped breathing. I quickly jumped up, pulled J.D. out of his chair, wrapped my arms around his midsection, and started performing the Heimlich. People were calling 911, the kids were all crying, and everybody was freaking out. It was chaos. It took a good three or four minutes for whatever had gotten stuck in his throat to dislodge and for J.D. to come back around. I tell you, I have never been so frightened in my entire life. I honestly thought we were going to lose him right then and there. If that had happened, on my watch and in front of his kids, I never would have been able to forgive myself.

It didn't strike me until much later, but right after that happened, I distinctly remember thanking God for stepping in and sparing J.D.'s life that day. I'm still grateful for that.

Another time, J.D. and I were over at the high school watching Jackson and Miller's football practice. It was just something we used to do together when J.D. was still able to get around without too much trouble. Usually, there was nobody else there, and we'd just sit in the stands by ourselves watching the boys practice. On this particular day, as practice was winding to a close, I turned to J.D. and said, "Let's go down to the field and talk with the coach while the boys get cleaned up."

As soon as I said that, J.D. stood up, and I'm still not sure what happened, but somehow he got his legs tangled up and started falling headlong into the row in front of us. Luckily, I got my leg in front of him and was able to intercept him with my arm before he fell. These were those old metal bleachers, so if he had hit his head, there's no telling how badly he could have gotten hurt. As soon as I scooped him up, I said, "J.D., are you okay?" Because of the progression of his illness, he wasn't able to show any emotion at the time, but man, my heart was beating right out of my chest. Nobody else was close enough to help, and I had almost missed catching him. I'm not going to lie, it shook me. *Lord*, I prayed under my breath, *thank you for taking care of us.*

As I was getting J.D. settled back down, I noticed another father sitting at the far end of the bleachers. As soon as we made eye contact, he stood up and made his way over to where we were sitting.

"Hey, Coach," he said. "I saw what just happened. That was a close one. It's a good thing you were there. Anyway, I just wanted to let you know that my family and I are praying for you and J.D. all the time."

"Thank you," I said. "I appreciate that." He just smiled at J.D. and me and quietly walked away.

You know, there were plenty of times during J.D.'s illness when I felt as though I was alone. But thinking back on that afternoon, I know now that I wasn't. Not only was God watching over J.D. and me, giving me the strength I needed and keeping him safe, but there were also a lot of other people out there—many of whom we never even met—thinking about us and praying for us. And if I may be so bold as to borrow from the great psalmist David, "Were I to count them," I expect "they would outnumber the grains of sand" (see Psalm 139:18).

God Was There

I spent so much of J.D.'s illness wondering where God was and why he refused to show up when we needed Him the most. But the truth is, He was there all along; I just didn't see it. He may not have shown up in the way I wanted, in the form of healing, but make no mistake, He did show up. He showed up when I was alone with J.D. on a high school football field. He showed up when I was with J.D. and my grandkids at that restaurant. And He showed up in front of millions of people at the Daytona 500.

Later, when I was doing my study to answer my questions about J.D.'s illness, a pastor friend of mine brought a passage to my attention that I had never thought about in regard to the questions I had. But if ever there was a passage that answers the question "Why didn't God show up?" this is it.

It comes from Psalm 139. Let's just look at what the psalmist David has to tell us about God here:

> You have searched me, LORD,
>   and you know me.
> You know when I sit and when I rise;
>   you perceive my thoughts from afar.
> You discern my going out and my lying down;
>   you are familiar with all my ways.
> Before a word is on my tongue
>   you, LORD, know it completely.
> You hem me in behind and before,
>   and you lay your hand upon me.
> Such knowledge is too wonderful for me,
>   too lofty for me to attain.
>
> PSALM 139:1-6

Basically, what David is saying here is that God knows everything about us—what we're thinking, what we're doing, and why we're doing it. How is that possible if He's not always there? In fact, the very next section assures us that He *is* always with us:

Where can I go from your Spirit?
Where can I flee from your presence?
If I go up to the heavens, you are there;
if I make my bed in the depths,
you are there.
If I rise on the wings of the dawn,
if I settle on the far side of the sea,
even there your hand will guide me,
your right hand will hold me fast.
If I say, "Surely the darkness will hide me
and the light become night around me,"
even the darkness will not be dark to you;
the night will shine like the day,
for darkness is as light to you.

PSALM 139:7-12

In other words, we couldn't get away from God if we tried. And that's not even the best part. For me, the next section says it all:

For you created my inmost being;
you knit me together in my mother's womb.
I praise you because I am fearfully and
wonderfully made;
your works are wonderful,
I know that full well.

My frame was not hidden from you
  when I was made in the secret place,
  when I was woven together in the depths
    of the earth.
Your eyes saw my unformed body;
  all the days ordained for me were written
    in your book
  before one of them came to be.
How precious to me are your thoughts, God!
  How vast is the sum of them!
Were I to count them,
  they would outnumber the grains of
    sand—
  when I awake, I am still with you.

PSALM 139:13-18

Not only does God know us, He knows *every-thing* about us and everything that was ever going to happen to us before he even made us.

Before J.D. was even born—heck, before Pat and I ever even met—God knew who J.D. was and exactly what was going to happen to him. He was there when J.D. was chasing that little orange puck around the gymnasium floor. He was there when J.D. met Melissa. He was there when we got J.D.'s diagnosis. He was there every minute of those five long years, holding J.D. in His right hand the entire time.

Angels All around Us

I said earlier that God gave J.D. the perfect wife in Melissa. Not only did she take wonderful care of J.D. during his illness, but she also taught me about what it looks like when God shows up. Just before I took the stage to lead everybody in prayer at J.D.'s memorial service, Melissa delivered a special message to those who were closest to J.D.—and, as it turns out, to me. Here's what she said:

> I want to take the opportunity to thank you all for the ways that you've cared for us in recent years. So many of you would have gladly carried this burden for us for a spell if you could, but since that wasn't possible, you found other ways to serve us. You prayed harder than I did. You baked. You cooked. You carpooled. You invested in my kids. You wrote letters, sent cards, bought gifts, traveled long distances to visit, and you wanted to know how we were really doing—even when you knew that answer would be hard to hear. You

never backed away because of the sadness or the awkwardness of our life. You showed up and you stayed to the end.

To J.D.'s friends, you've shown my boys the most beautiful example of friendship that I can imagine, and when they want to remember their dad, they only have to look to you. He chose his friends very well. To the outstanding group of people who cared for J.D., including many doctors who provided personal cell phone numbers, made house calls, checked in after hours; and the caregivers, hospice nurses, and therapists who cared for J.D. like a family member—you are the reason that we had as much time as we did. The level of compassion you had for J.D. when he couldn't reciprocate a bit of it kept us afloat. Caregivers, your job was excruciatingly difficult, and I'll never be able to thank you enough for linking arms with me.

With sickness like this, it's easy to ask the question, "Where is God?" But I know where He was. He was in you. You were His hands and feet.

Like I said, sometimes God just gives a guy the perfect wife.

I guess what I'm trying to say is, there may be times when it feels like God's not there. Like He's not listening. Or like He simply doesn't care. But I'm here to tell you, nothing could be further from the truth. He's there in the form of friends and family who reach out to us in our darkest hours and in those who offer a kind word, a helping hand, or a shoulder to cry on when we need it most.

He knows everything about us. He knows everything that's happening in our lives. And He knows the reasons why. We may not always be able to understand those reasons, but He does, and at the end of the day, that's all that matters.

And believe me, God understands grief. He knows what it feels like to watch someone you love suffer. He knows what it feels like to lose a Son. He knows what you're going through, and He is with you as you go through it.

We just have to have the faith and the confidence that no matter what happens, God is never going to leave us. His presence may not always look the way we hope it will. But rest assured, He will always show up.

3
"ARE WE JUST LIVING A LIFE OF CHANCE?"

FROM 1981 TO 1992, I basically lived in a little two-story brick building a couple miles off Dulles Toll Road in Chantilly, Virginia. That was the old Redskins Park, the training facility of the Washington Redskins, and roughly 120 hours a week—including most nights and weekends—my home as well.

During my tenure as head coach, I probably spent more time at Redskins Park than I did with Pat and the boys, and though I deeply regret that now, at the time it was just what I felt like I had to do to develop a winning formula.

You see, as I mentioned earlier, one of the

most important things a football coach does every week is to create the game plan.[1] So every week, I would hole up in my office with my assistant coaches for hours, drafting and redrafting our game plan for the following Sunday. We would think through every play from every angle, taking into account—as best we could—every possible situation. Are we playing indoors or outdoors? What's the weather supposed to be like? Who's healthy, who's injured? We thought through every down and every yardage situation, on what downs and distances we might see man, zone, or blitz. Our game plan was so detailed that it even divided the red zone into five-yard increments, with specific plays for each segment.

Out of hundreds of plays and dozens of formations, my coaches and I picked the best ones for each game and each situation. We planned for every possible eventuality, and we didn't leave anything to chance.

And the same thing goes for racing. If we think the race is going to come down to fuel mileage, our strategy takes into account when we will pit to take on fuel. We also have a tire strategy. We might change two tires sometimes, as opposed to all four. Obviously, the car gains a lot of track position with a shorter pit stop, but we have to weigh that against tire wear and performance.

Likewise, there are four basic track types in the NASCAR Cup Series: short tracks, intermediates, superspeedways, and road courses. Does that matter? You bet it does. It means a whole different car setup if we're racing at Talladega, a superspeedway with speeds near 200 miles per hour, or at Watkins Glen, a road course where we have to worry about the brakes overheating. Different type of track? Different game plan.

If you are in the running for a championship at the end of the year, finishing high is more important than risking everything to win. You are not going to take the chance of running out of gas to win a race. On the other hand, if you don't have a shot at the championship, you have nothing to lose. You might say, "We're going to stretch our gas mileage and skip the last pit stop to try and win this race." You get the picture.

Now, if we go to such great lengths to make sure every possible outcome is anticipated and accounted for, doesn't it stand to reason that God—our heavenly Father, who loves us so much He sent His own Son to die on a cross so we could be forgiven—would do the same for us?

Seems like kind of a no-brainer, doesn't it? And yet, when J.D. got sick, I genuinely questioned whether some things in life, well . . . just happen.

Do Things Just Happen?

Okay, so we've established that there are hundreds of decisions that go into every football game and NASCAR race—some of them big, some of them small, but all of them vital to the outcome.

In life, the first "big" decision I ever had to make was when I was eight years old. I was in the third grade—right in the center of the Bible Belt, mind you—and my teacher was telling me how two billion years ago, two amoebas just happened to hit in a muddy puddle of water somewhere, and I was the result. Now, I wasn't the sharpest knife in the drawer, but that didn't make sense even to me. I mean, that teacher was basically telling me that I was an accident! My pastor, on the other hand, was telling me something completely different. He told me that there was an all-knowing, all-loving, all-powerful God who "knit me together in my mother's womb" (Psalm 139:13), that He made me unique and special, and that He wanted to have a personal relationship with me.

Not only was what my pastor was saying a lot more attractive, it also made a lot more sense. I knew I was no accident. I mean, think about the world and the way it's put together. Earth is tilted at just the right angle and spinning at just the right speed, just close enough to the sun to sustain life. There are plants and trees putting off oxygen so you and I can breathe. Things like that simply don't happen by accident.

So for me, that first big decision was easy. I went forward in church and said, "God, I know I'm not an accident. I know you made me, and I want to have a personal relationship with you." That was the most important decision I have ever made in my life. It was a decision to trust that things do not just happen by chance.

Does God Really Care?

We've already established that God knows everything about us—even before we're born. The next question is, does God *care* about what happens to us?

When I was coaching the Redskins, I genuinely cared about our players. Granted, some of them could be difficult to work with, but I always cared about them, and I felt like it was my job to help them become the best football players they could possibly be. Same with the race team. Yes, winning is important, but I care about our drivers, their safety, and their success in the sport.

I have said many times before that the greatest gift Pat and I have ever been given was our two boys. When J.D. and Coy came into the world, it changed my whole life. For the first time, I wasn't focused solely on myself (sorry, Pat). I would have done anything to protect them and to make sure they had whatever they needed to be happy and to succeed. Any father would.

Well, God is our heavenly Father, and in His Word, it says, "God so loved the world that he gave his one and only Son, that whoever believes in him shall not perish but have eternal life" (John 3:16). If that isn't love, I honestly don't know what is.

So not only does God know what will happen to us, He cares about what happens to us and wants what is best for us because He loves us as His children.

Is There a Plan?

You might be wondering why God would let His only Son go through everything that He did. After all, Jesus was without sin. He wasn't deserving of any of the pain or suffering He endured. Frankly, I wondered the same thing when J.D. got sick. Now, J.D. wasn't perfect, but he lived such a godly life—always looking out for others, always trying to be the best husband, father, brother, and friend he could be—it just made me question, why did this happen? Does God control what happens to us, or do bad things just happen to us by chance? I mean, I've been involved in professional sports long enough to know that sometimes the breaks naturally go your way and sometimes they don't. But does that same principle extend to life as well?

After J.D. went home to be with the Lord, I spent a lot of time studying the Bible to find an answer to that question. In addition to Psalm 139, here's what I found.

Proverbs 16:33 says, "The lot is cast into the lap, but its every decision is from the Lord." In other words, we might be the ones throwing the dice, but God determines how they fall. I really like this picture because I can't think of a better example of random luck than a roll of the dice. And this verse makes it clear that God is in control even of that.

Likewise, Proverbs 16:9 tells us, "We can make our plans, but the LORD determines our steps" (NLT). In other words, we can get it into our heads what we would like to do, but ultimately God is going to lead us where He wants us to go.

And in Isaiah 14:24, the Lord says, "It will all happen as I have planned. It will be as I have decided" (NLT). I think that one speaks for itself.

By the way, in case you're wondering, the Bible itself didn't come about by chance either— it couldn't have. How do I know? Do you know that party game Telephone, where one person makes up a sentence and tells it to another person, and then they pass it on to another, and so on and so on until it eventually makes its way all the way around the room, and by the fourth or fifth person, it doesn't even make any sense anymore?

Back when I was the offensive coordinator for the Buccaneers, we didn't have helmet mics like they have today, so we developed a system of hand signals from the sidelines to tell our quarterback out on the field which play to call. He would then tell the team in the huddle. It was an effective way for me to call the plays and communicate them to the team.

Unfortunately, we lost the first two games of the season.

So Coach McKay came to me and said, "Joe, I'm not comfortable with these hand signals. I want you to tell a player on the sideline, who'll go in and tell the quarterback, who'll tell the team. That way, I'll be able to hear you, and it'll be better than using these signals I don't know anything about."

When we lost a couple more games, Coach McKay came to me again and said, "Joe, I don't think you're comfortable being on the sidelines calling these plays. I want you to go upstairs to the press box and call the play down to an assistant coach on the sideline, who'll tell a player, who will tell the quarterback, who will tell the team."

Now, I'm here to tell you, when you send a play call like "trips-right-zoom-liz-585-F-cross-sneak" to a receiver who has already been hit in the head three or four times, you shouldn't be surprised if you have some trouble recognizing the play when the ball is snapped.

Now stop to consider that the Bible was written by more than forty different authors across two continents in three different languages over a period of 1,500 years and has shown itself to be perfect from Genesis to Revelation. I mean, the Old Testament has over three hundred predictions that were fulfilled when Christ came to this earth, lived the perfect life, went to the cross, was crucified, and went back to heaven—more than four hundred years after it was written! Something like that doesn't just happen by chance. God orchestrated that. So when the Bible tells us, "It will all happen as [God has] planned," believe me, you can take that to the bank.

Blind Spots

Here's where things get a little complicated. Jeremiah 29:11 tells us, "'I know the plans I have for you,' declares the LORD, 'plans to prosper you and not to harm you, plans to give you hope and a future.'" If this is true—and I believe it is—then why did God allow J.D. to get sick and to leave us all so early? I just couldn't make sense of it.

I spoke with a pastor friend of mine about it. He told me that when he was a kid, he used to watch his favorite college football team practice every day after school. Even back in those days, team practices were closed to the public, but my friend found a little knothole in the fence that surrounded the field, and he used to get up on his tiptoes and look through that hole to watch the team practice. The problem was, he could only see a tiny bit of what was happening— basically whatever was right in front of him. Obviously, there was a lot more going on behind that fence than what he was looking at. He just couldn't see it.

Our drivers experience a similar phenom- enon on race days. Our cars don't have tradi- tional side mirrors, so their view is limited. But we have spotters at the top of the racetrack, and they communicate with our drivers to help them avoid trouble.

The point is, in our lives here on earth, we can only see a little bit—essentially, what's right in front of us. But God sees everything—even things that haven't happened yet.

When I think about J.D.'s illness from an earthly perspective, it seems utterly random. But when I think about all the letters and e-mails we received after the Daytona 500 from people who dedicated their lives to Christ, and all the men who told me they were going to start spending more time with their kids after listening to J.D.'s boys talk at his memorial service, I now believe that God, in His infinite wisdom, allowed this to happen to J.D. because He knew the impact it would have on others. He could see the full picture. I couldn't—then. But I see better now. In fact, I think it's still too early to see all the amazing and wonderful ways J.D.'s life will honor the Lord. I'm already seeing hints of it in his boys, and I expect J.D.'s life will continue to impact people long after I'm with him in heaven. I'll tell you one thing—it will sure be fun to watch.

Take Heart

When someone we love gets sick or leaves us, it's tempting to chalk it up to bad luck, chance, or fate. But I believe God is sovereign. I believe He created us, He loves us, and He has a unique plan for each and every one of us that extends far beyond anything we have the capacity to see or understand. From time to time, sickness and suffering may come into our lives, and though it may feel like just bad luck, it's all part of His plan. Our job is to trust Him and to believe.

In Genesis 50:20, after enduring great suffering at the hands of his brothers, Joseph says to them, "You intended to harm me, but God intended it all for good. He brought me to this position so I could save the lives of many people" (NLT). I believe God similarly used what J.D. suffered to benefit many others. And I believe He is doing the same thing through countless other believers every day.

Why did God allow His own Son to suffer and die? I believe it is for the same reason He allowed J.D. to go through what he went through. He knew the endgame.

As Jesus himself said in John 16:33, "I have told you all this so that you may have peace in me. Here on earth you will have many trials and sorrows. But take heart, because I have overcome the world" (NLT). Jesus' suffering and death was the way he overcame the world for our benefit.

So are we just living a life of chance? Absolutely not. The planet we are living on did not happen by accident. *We* are not here by accident. And the Bible did not happen by accident either. Our lives are not left to chance. God is in control. He can see the whole picture, while we see only a small part. He loves us, He knows what's best for us, and our role is to trust Him with our limited perspective.

4
"WHY DO CHRISTIANS SUFFER?"

I KNOW WHAT YOU'RE THINKING. "Hey, Coach, if God loves us as much as you say He does, then why is there suffering at all?" That's a great question. In fact, I asked that very same question a lot during J.D.'s illness.

It all goes back to the Garden of Eden. I'm sure you've heard this story. To begin with, at the start of the Bible, in the very first chapter of Genesis, we are told that everything God created—the earth, the sky, the waters, the plants, the trees—was all "very good" (Genesis 1:31). That's important to remember. God created Adam and Eve and put them in a garden filled with everything they could possibly need. There was only one rule—they were not to eat from the tree of the knowledge of good and evil. Well, you know what happened next. The serpent convinced Eve to eat from the tree, and then she gave some of that fruit to Adam. God showed up and asked them what happened (even though He knew). Adam blamed Eve, Eve blamed the serpent, and God said,

> Cursed is the ground because of you;
> > through painful toil you will eat food from it
> > all the days of your life.
> It will produce thorns and thistles for you,
> > and you will eat the plants of the field.
> By the sweat of your brow
> > you will eat your food
> until you return to the ground,
> > since from it you were taken;
> for dust you are
> > and to dust you will return.

GENESIS 3:17-19

Then God banished them both from the Garden and put an angel on guard to make sure they couldn't get back in. And that was it.

God created a perfect, beautiful, idyllic world for us to live in, and by disobeying God, Adam and Eve let sin and suffering in. And we've been living in a fallen world ever since. The point is, God didn't bring sin and suffering into the world. *We* did. That was our choice.

God did not make J.D. sick. Sickness and death came about as a result of the Fall.

Reading God's Will

Usually when something tragic happens, pastors will point you toward Romans 8:28: "We know that in all things God works for the good of those who love him, who have been called according to his purpose." In other words, we don't have to worry; somehow, God is going to cause something good to come out of even our tragic circumstances.

Now, while I do believe that God used J.D.'s illness to call others to Christ, as I studied the book of Romans a little more, I was struck by what it says a few verses earlier:

> The Spirit himself testifies with our spirit that we are God's children. Now if we are children, then we are heirs—heirs of God

and co-heirs with Christ, if indeed we
share in his sufferings in order that we
may also share in his glory.

ROMANS 8:16-17

Okay. We know that Jesus Christ was the Son
of God. When we give our life to Christ, God
becomes our Father, and we become fellow
heirs with Christ. And what do heirs get? Heirs
get everything the Father gets.

Believe it or not, in Christ's day, if you were a
natural-born son, your father could opt to cast
you out. He could deny that you were, by birth,
his son and in doing so deny you your inheritance. But if you were to go through the adoption
process, legally, there was no way that a father
could ever say you were not his son. Well, when
we accept Christ as our Lord and Savior, we are,
in effect, adopted children of God and heirs with
Christ.

So, back to Romans. If we are indeed
coheirs with Christ, then we can expect to
receive everything that He received. And
what did Christ receive? He received two
things—"sufferings" and "glory." Let's take a
closer look at that.

Suffering

At some point, everyone endures suffering. Our family is certainly no exception.

Back when I was coaching with the Chargers, Pat suffered an acoustic neuroma, which is a tumor behind the ear. She had been slowly losing her hearing in her left ear for several years, but she didn't want to bother me with it during the season, so she kept it to herself. By the time it was officially diagnosed, the tumor had grown to the size of a golf ball. The good news was, it wasn't cancerous. However, the surgery to remove the tumor carried with it a lot of risks.

The four hours Pat spent in surgery were some of the longest of my life. I knew the doctors had performed this operation hundreds of times before and in twenty years had lost only one patient due to unexpected hemorrhaging, but knowing that there was even a slight possibility that our boys might have to grow up without their mother was almost more than I could handle.

The operation went well, or so we thought. While Pat was in recovery, the doctors noticed some unexpected bleeding and wheeled her back into surgery. I was beside myself. Pat was such a strong, loving, and generous woman. I couldn't understand why this was happening to her.

Fortunately, the doctors were able to stop the bleeding. However, Pat suffered partial paralysis of her face and was unable to close her left eye. She had to stay in the hospital for two more weeks and undergo another procedure to install a spring-loaded clip in her eyelid so she could close it again.

Pat has always been a beautiful woman. In fact, people used to come up to me in restaurants and tell me how gorgeous she was. After that surgery, she struggled greatly with her appearance, to the point where she could barely bring herself to look in a mirror.

She still has problems with her eyes and has a few balance issues, and she's been dealing with them for going on forty years now. She has also endured two big back surgeries and a knee replacement, all of which she handled with grace, dignity, and an unfailing faith in the Lord. I'm telling you, Pat is without a doubt one of the strongest, most beautiful women I have ever met. And yet she suffered.

In January 2007, when J.D. and Melissa's fourth son, Taylor, was just two years old, he became seriously ill. The doctors feared leukemia. I'll never forget waiting for the final diagnosis and seeing older kids in the hospital who were suffering from what we dreaded Taylor might have. We paced and prayed and cried and hoped. And even though we had been warned to be prepared, when the leukemia diagnosis was confirmed, we were devastated.

Precious Taylor underwent operations and chemotherapy. If anything will test your faith or make you want to question God, it's when a little loved one suffers like that. I can't say I understand it, and I sure don't like it. But I've learned the true meaning of intercessory prayer. It isn't just praying for someone; it's being willing to trade places with him or her and wishing you could.

I myself suffer from diabetes, no doubt triggered by my lifestyle, my eating habits, my age, and maybe some genetics. Half of those I could have controlled. But when a toddler gets a horrific disease . . . that is just incredibly difficult to understand.

I am happy to report that as of this writing,

Taylor is cancer-free and just celebrated his sixteenth birthday. But there were definitely some dark days in the Gibbs family while he was fighting.

And of course, J.D. endured five long years of suffering from a horrible, debilitating disease that slowly stripped him of everything. I mean, this guy was a star—athletic, not an ounce of fat on him, always out running, biking, swimming, skiing—and in the end, he couldn't even move.

But nobody on this earth suffered more than Jesus. He did absolutely nothing wrong, yet He was falsely accused, betrayed, arrested, mocked, lashed, beaten, spit upon, and nailed to a cross. I won't get into the details, just suffice it to say, crucifixion is one of the most gruesome and brutal ways that you can imagine to execute someone. And again, Jesus did absolutely nothing wrong. So why should we, who brought sin and suffering into the world, expect to be immune from it?

There's a great verse in 1 Peter that addresses this very thing. It says, "Dear friends, don't be surprised at the fiery trials you are going through, as if something strange were happening to you." I love that. But then he goes right into the second part of our inheritance. He says, "Instead, be very glad—for these trials make you partners with Christ in his suffering, so that you will have the wonderful joy of seeing his glory" (1 Peter 4:12-13, NLT). Basically, what the apostle Peter is saying here is that instead of being surprised or upset that we have to endure suffering, we should be grateful, because that means, as followers of Christ, we've got something much better coming our way.

Glory

We started this chapter by talking about Romans 8:16-17. So we know that when we accept Christ as our Lord and Savior, we are officially welcomed into God's family and will therefore inherit everything from Him that Christ inherited. We know that this means suffering. But look what comes in the very next verse: "I consider that our present sufferings are not worth comparing with the glory that will be revealed in us" (Romans 8:18). In other words, no matter how bad our current suffering is, it is nothing compared to the glory that is waiting for us in heaven.

Why is that? Well, for one thing, one of the promises of heaven is that there is no more suffering. Revelation 21:4 tells us that God "will wipe every tear from [our] eyes. There will be no more death or mourning or crying or pain, for the old order of things has passed away."

At the end of his life, J.D. couldn't walk, he couldn't swallow, he couldn't communicate—he had everything taken away from him. But today, I believe J.D. can have a great meal, go for a run, and have a conversation with his friends, and he'll never have to suffer again.

While this is what I believe, I wanted to be sure, so I called my good friend Randy Alcorn, who is one of the world's foremost scholars on the subject of heaven. Here's what he told me.

J.D. loved to work out and challenge and strengthen his body. As strong as his body once was on this old earth, his resurrection body will be a major upgrade! Even now, before his resurrection, J.D. is already sinless and full of love, his mind is brilliant and insightful. In fact— and I love this—the Bible speaks of people now in heaven talking, walking, gathering, singing, worshiping, praying, falling on their knees, wearing clothes, wearing crowns and then casting them at the feet of Jesus, and even "holding palm branches in their hands" (Revelation 7:9).

Some think this is all figurative, but considering that from the beginning God created humans to be both physical and spiritual (see Genesis 2:7), there's another explanation. Some theologians believe that right now heaven is in fact a physical place and that God may grant His people temporary physical forms, sort of bridging the gap from this life to our eternal life, so we still retain a semblance of our full humanity prior to the resurrection. That's what I envision as I think about J.D. now.

J.D. wasn't one to just sit around doing nothing. I believe right now he's active and creative, engaging with God, serving Him in heaven, learning new things, and enjoying great friendships, both old and new, with people and maybe angels, too. Since all of us will give an account of our lives when we stand before God (see Romans 14:12), our memories in the afterlife will have to be better than now, not worse. We'll surely remember the things we did and the people we spent our lives with. Will J.D. and I recognize each other? Of course! We will all be smarter in Heaven, not dumber!

God promises us that when we die, we "will receive a rich welcome into the eternal kingdom of our Lord and Savior Jesus Christ" (2 Peter 1:11). Jesus Himself will welcome us, and wouldn't it be fitting if those we most love and miss will be part of our welcoming committee in heaven? Won't they be among the very first to greet us when we enter heaven? I expect J.D. to be in my welcoming committee, and I hope right now he's picking out things to do, places to go, and people to see that he's going to share with his dad when I get there!

While J.D. has experienced heaven before me, I love the promise that one day, after the resurrection, he and I and all of God's people will at the same time go to the New Earth, enjoying and exploring it together, to the glory of God! We will worship, work, and play together, enjoying the wonders of His new creation through new eyes. That will be the greatest adventure in human history, and it's a great comfort knowing that my son and I and the rest of my family who know Jesus—and you too if you know Him—will all experience it together! Think about it—this isn't a fairy tale; it's the blood-bought promise of Jesus that if we trust Him for the salvation He purchased for us, we really *will* all live happily ever after!

Which leads me to the second point about God's glory and why our earthly suffering can't compare. Our suffering, though painful, is only temporary. God's glory is eternal.

Christ went through suffering. Now Christ is sitting at the right hand of the Lord, reigning in glory forever. J.D. suffered for five years, and yes, it was long and painful. But now, J.D. is with Christ and enjoying that eternal glory. And as much as I miss J.D., I can find peace in that.

Ticket to Paradise

The reason suffering exists is because we live in a fallen world. We live in a fallen world because, given the choice between obedience and rebellion, Adam and Eve chose rebellion. God didn't want the world to be the way it is now—full of pain and sickness and misery and despair. That's not the way He made it. He gave us Paradise. We made it a mess. But He also gave us a way to get back to glory.

I've mentioned this verse before, but it bears repeating. In fact, if you go to almost any football game or NASCAR race—especially in the South—odds are you'll see someone in the stands holding up a sign that reads "John 3:16."

Here's what that verse says: "For God so loved the world that he gave his one and only Son, that whoever believes in him shall not perish but have eternal life." Accepting Christ makes us heirs with Christ, and we receive everything Christ received—suffering, yes, but also glory. And glory is forever.

5
"WHY DO SOME CHRISTIANS SUFFER MORE THAN OTHERS?"

DURING THE LAST WEEKS of J.D.'s life, I finally accepted that he was not going to win his battle. I've known quite a few people who were taken home too soon. Sean Taylor, our Pro Bowl safety with the Redskins, was only twenty-four when he died of a gunshot wound to the leg back in 2007. Pro golfer Payne Stewart was just forty-two when he died in a plane crash. And Dale Earnhardt Sr. was only forty-nine, the same age as J.D., when he lost his life in a wreck during the final lap at the 2001 Daytona 500.

Part of what made those losses so tragic was that they all happened so suddenly. There was no warning, no time to prepare, and no opportunity to say goodbye. We watched J.D. battle his disease for five years. Our family was all with him when he went to be with the Lord. And I can tell you, it didn't make it any easier. In fact, for me, it made it even harder. I was resigned to the fact that God was going to take J.D. home, but what I couldn't understand was why God was letting him go through such a long, painful struggle. Why didn't He just take him home right away? Why does God allow some people to suffer so much more than others?

As I thought about that question, two people from the Bible sprang to mind—Job and Paul.

Job

Prior to Christ's arrival, it's hard to imagine anyone in the Bible who suffered more than Job. Job was a wealthy farmer who lived back in Old Testament times. He had a lot of property and livestock, a house full of servants, and a large family and was a highly respected member of the community. He was also a man of great faith.

Now Satan believed that the reason Job had such strong faith was because God had given him so much. So one day, he challenged the Lord, saying, "Take away everything [Job] has, and he will surely curse you to your face!" (Job 1:11, NLT).

Because God was confident in Job's faith, He let Satan test him. Satan took everything away from Job—first his livestock, then his servants, and then even his children. All were destroyed. But still, Job remained faithful. Then Satan covered Job from head to toe with painful boils. Even his own wife told him it was time to give up on God. Bear in mind, at this point, Job was scratching his diseased skin with a broken piece of pottery and sitting in a heap of ashes. But Job remained faithful and said to her, "Should we accept only good things from the hand of God and never anything bad?" (Job 2:10, NLT).

So why did God let Job go through all of this? I believe the answer lies in Job 13:15. Even after everything had been taken from him, Job says, "Though [God] slay me, yet will I hope in him." Honestly, I think that is one of the greatest statements of faith in the Bible. For Job to go through so much pain and loss and still be able to say, "God, even if you kill me, I'm still yours" is a lot more than most people could say.

There's no question, Job was someone special. God knew that, and that's why He let Satan do what he did.

For whatever reason, some people are capable of handling more adversity than others, and I think that's why some *do* endure more. But it goes further than that. It's not just a question of how much suffering we can handle; it's also about how we handle it. When tragedy strikes, will we turn our backs on God, like Job's wife, or will we remain faithful to the Lord and trust that He has our best interests at heart—even if we can't yet see it?

God knew that Job was strong enough to handle these trials and that his faith in the face of such immense suffering was going to be a great witness to others. And it was. I have since claimed Job 13:15 for my own life, though to be honest, I'm not sure I could have handled everything Job faced in the way he handled it.

By the way, in the end, the Lord fully restored Job's fortune. The Bible tells us, "In fact, the LORD gave him twice as much as before!" (Job 42:10, NLT). He even blessed him with ten more children. Not only did Job love the Lord, the Lord loved him, too.

Paul

Another example of someone who endured great suffering is Paul. When we first meet Paul in the New Testament, he is actively persecuting Christians. But immediately following a personal encounter with Christ, Paul completely changed course and became one of the most devoted Christians in history. Not only did he travel thousands of miles preaching the Good News of Jesus, he wrote thirteen of the twenty-seven books in the New Testament.

Once Paul converted to Christianity, he faced a lot of the same persecution that he used to dole out himself. There are several books of the Bible dedicated to Paul's ministry, but this passage in 2 Corinthians does an excellent job of summarizing Paul's misfortunes:

> Five times I received from the Jews the forty lashes minus one. Three times I was beaten with rods, once I was pelted with stones, three times I was shipwrecked, I spent a night and a day in the open sea, I have been constantly on the move. I have been in danger from rivers, in

danger from bandits, in danger from
my fellow Jews, in danger from Gentiles;
in danger in the city, in danger in the
country, in danger at sea; and in danger
from false believers. I have labored and
toiled and have often gone without sleep;
I have known hunger and thirst and have
often gone without food; I have been cold
and naked.

2 CORINTHIANS 11:24-27

All Paul was doing was traveling from place to
place sharing the Good News, and for that he was
arrested, flogged, and beaten and spent more
than two and a half years in prison. But despite
all his suffering, Paul never once wavered in his
faith. He never once doubted God's love for him.
Paul even wrote a letter to the church in Rome
in which he asked, "Does it mean he no longer
loves us if we have trouble or calamity, or are
persecuted, or hungry, or destitute, or in danger, or threatened with death? . . . No, despite
all these things, overwhelming victory is ours
through Christ, who loved us" (Romans 8:35, 37,
NLT). He also wrote one of my favorite verses,
which we've already looked at: "We know that

in all things God works for the good of those who love him, who have been called according to his purpose" (Romans 8:28).

We'll talk about that verse a little more in the next chapter, but the fact that Paul was strong enough in his faith to say that God loved him and would take care of him despite everything he had been through is, I believe, one of the reasons God allowed him to endure so much suffering.

The point is, God knows who is capable of enduring great suffering and who isn't. And He knows who will use that suffering, not to question or deny Him, but as an opportunity to witness to others about His love.

To our discredit, we usually don't give God our attention unless we are uncomfortable. When things are going our way, we often overlook Him. C. S. Lewis wrote, "God whispers to us in our pleasures, speaks to us in our conscience, but shouts in our pain: it is His megaphone to rouse a deaf world."[1]

A Family Affair

God considered that Job and Paul were both strong enough to endure what they did. And I firmly believe He thought the same thing about J.D. God knew J.D. and his family, and He knew they would be a great witness through their adversity.

I include J.D.'s family in this because J.D.'s suffering didn't affect just him, and it was an opportunity for them to witness to God's character as well. The way those four boys looked after their dad right up to the end was nothing short of extraordinary. They were never embarrassed and never ashamed, and they never let their situation get them down. A lot of that was due to Melissa. I won't go into all the details. Suffice it to say, for five years, Melissa dealt with one unimaginable situation after another with incredible strength and grace. Through it all, she was a great witness and a powerful testimony—particularly to me and Pat, but also to everyone around her—of what unconditional love looks like.

Once, when Taylor was battling leukemia, Melissa said to me, "That's probably the reason why God put me here on this earth—to be there for him during this fight." When J.D. became sick, she realized Taylor's illness had prepared her for what was to come. Once again, God saw the big picture.

When You Get Knocked Down . . .

When J.D. went to be with the Lord, I spent a lot of time questioning why such a godly young man had to endure so much suffering. Now I realize that J.D. was allowed to suffer, in part, *because* he was such a godly young man.

God made J.D. He knew what he was capable of handling. He knew how strong J.D.'s faith was, how strong his wife was, and how strong his boys were. And He knew that as others watched them go through this difficult battle, they would see how much this family loved the Lord, even in the middle of all their suffering.

At the risk of giving the devil his due, I can see where he was coming from when he told God, "Look, of course Job loves you. You've given him everything. Let's see what happens when you take it all away." It is easy to have faith and to witness to others about how good the Lord is when things are going well. But it takes a special kind of person to keep on doing it when things aren't going so well. God knows who those people are. They haven't been singled out for punishment. They have been chosen to fulfill a great mission.

The Good with the Bad

Sometimes it feels like God distributes blessings and difficulties unevenly, or even unfairly. Goodness knows, our family has been very blessed. But we've also seen our share of suffering. It's important to remember that our job is to be good stewards of both—the good and the bad.

In the book of Luke, Jesus tells us, "From everyone who has been given much, much will be demanded; and from the one who has been entrusted with much, much more will be asked" (Luke 12:48). That goes both ways.

When God gives us great blessings—like wealth or position—He expects us to use those blessings, not for our own benefit, but for the benefit of others. Likewise, when suffering comes our way, God doesn't want us to wallow in despair. He wants us to use that suffering as a means of witnessing and ministering to others.

I'd like to close this chapter with one last verse from Paul. I've given a lot of halftime speeches in my day, many of them when we were behind and struggling. I think what Paul says here is a great message to anyone who's thinking, *I don't know if I can do this.* Believe me when I say, with God, you can:

> We are pressed on every side by troubles, but not crushed and broken. We are perplexed because we don't know why things happen as they do, but we don't give up and quit. We are hunted down, but God never abandons us. We get knocked down, but we get up again and keep going. These bodies of ours are constantly facing death just as Jesus did; so it is clear to all that it is only the living Christ within who keeps us safe.
>
> 2 CORINTHIANS 4:8-10, TLB

6
"DO WE REALLY REAP WHAT WE SOW?"

BACK IN 2015, KYLE BUSCH, who drives our #18 M&M/Interstate Batteries car, got into a terrible wreck in an Xfinity Series race in Daytona. It was the 113th lap, and Kyle was trying to push one of our other drivers through the middle of the pack, when he veered off the track and slammed into the concrete retaining wall going 90 miles per hour.

Fortunately, Kyle was able to hit the brakes enough to slow the car down from its original speed, but because both of his feet were pressed down on the brake pedal when he hit the wall, he suffered a compound fracture of his right leg and crushed his left foot.

I was there at the hospital that night while he was waiting to go into surgery, and believe me when I tell you, that was one gruesome injury.

The doctors in Daytona put a steel rod in his leg to fix the fracture, then we flew him back to Charlotte, where the doctors performed the surgery on his foot. They didn't give any time-table for recovery, but given his condition, we expected him to miss the whole season. Two years earlier, one of our other drivers, Tony Stewart, broke his leg in a wreck at Southern Iowa Speedway, and it took him about six months to fully recover.

But Kyle was determined to get back that sea-son. He started rehabbing right away, and as soon as he was able to stand up, he was working out like crazy. We have a weight room at JGR that our pit crew guys use to stay in shape during the season, and as much as those guys hustle, I don't know that I've ever seen anyone work as hard as Kyle did that spring.

Not only did he make it back that season, but he did it in eleven weeks. Mind you, Kyle struggled just to walk again. The first time he tried to stand up, the pain was so bad that he almost blacked out. But he kept at it, and all that hard work and determination paid off. Kyle won five of his final races that season *and* the Sprint Cup Series Championship.

Right-Hand Man

For most of my adult life, I have firmly believed in the promises of two passages from Scripture. The first, which we have already discussed, is Romans 8:28: "We know that in all things God works for the good of those who love him, who have been called according to his purpose." The other is Galatians 6:7-10:

> Do not be deceived: God cannot be mocked. A man reaps what he sows. Whoever sows to please their flesh, from the flesh will reap destruction; whoever sows to please the Spirit, from the Spirit will reap eternal life. Let us not become weary in doing good, for at the proper time we will reap a harvest if we do not give up. Therefore, as we have opportunity, let us do good to all people, especially to those who belong to the family of believers.

After J.D. went home, I started studying sermons by respected pastors on the subject of reaping what you sow, and what jumped out at me as I listened to the likes of Billy Graham and Alistair Begg was that they were all basically saying the same thing: "If you do good things, you're going to get good things in return." But the more I thought about J.D., the more I thought, *That doesn't add up.* J.D. had always lived such a godly life and was always helping people. His illness and premature death didn't seem to be reaping what he sowed.

I remember one time while J.D. was sick, Melissa had to take a trip. At that point, J.D. pretty much required round-the-clock care, so we took him up to a nearby hospice facility for two nights. I stayed with him one night, and then my assistant, Cindy, stayed with him for the other. Anyway, the night I was staying with him, the nurse came in to see me, and she said, "Joe, I don't know if you're aware of this, but when J.D. was healthy, he used to come up here and talk to all of the patients."

I had no idea he did that.

Shortly after J.D. went home to be with the Lord, a young woman sent me a letter along with a picture of herself in a wheelchair. She said that she came to the JGR complex one day to look around. J.D. saw her, came downstairs, and took her on a tour of the whole building. She closed the letter by saying, "I'm writing you this note to tell you I miss him. That day is something I'll always remember."

Once again, I had no idea.

We had a guy who worked for us part-time. He lived several hours away, so he would just come in on race weekends. Typically, we travel by plane. It's a lot faster and easier, and in the end, it makes more sense economically. Well, one night, after the planes landed back at the complex, J.D. noticed this guy getting on his motorbike and said, "What are you doing?" The guy replied, "Well, I don't want you guys to have to pay for an extra flight, so I just ride my bike home from here." Mind you, this guy lived over a hundred miles away. Well, the very next day, he got a letter from J.D. that said, "You're never going to take that motorbike back and forth again. You're flying, and we'll take care of you."

I think that's where J.D. was really different from me. I speak to big crowds. I write books, and I do TV interviews. It's all very public. That's my ministry. That's what God has given me. But J.D. dealt with people on an individual level, and a lot of the time, nobody except the person he was helping even knew he was doing it.

Jesus says in the Sermon on the Mount, "When you give to the needy, do not let your left hand know what your right hand is doing, so that your giving may be in secret" (Matthew 6:3-4). That's what J.D. did.

The piece I was struggling with was what comes next: "Then your Father, who sees what is done in secret, will reward you" (Matthew 6:4). J.D. had done so much good—much of it in private. Where was his reward?

As it turns out, the answer had been staring me in the face the whole time.

Standing Room Only

When J.D. went home, Melissa arranged for his memorial service to be held at Davidson College's Belk Arena, not only because she and J.D. were season ticket holders for the Davidson basketball team, but also because it was the only venue in the area that could accommodate the number of people who wanted to celebrate J.D.'s life. There were over three thousand people there that day. And every person in attendance represented a life J.D. had touched.

Melissa planned the whole service in the hope that it would lead people to Christ. Everything about it—the speakers, the music, J.D.'s boys reading excerpts from his daily log—was a testimony to J.D.'s love for the Lord. Melissa even commented in her opening remarks that "if [this service] turns into a full-on revival, nothing would please him more."

And that's exactly what it did.

I can't tell you how many people came up to me afterward to tell me they gave their lives to Christ during that service. Since then, we've received countless letters and e-mails from people who made the same commitment after watching the service online. J.D. dedicated his whole life to being a godly influence and leading others to Christ. Those were the seeds he sowed. And in the end, God gave J.D. the best reward He possibly could—a front-row seat from heaven to watch the harvest as one person after another dedicated their lives to Christ because of him.

Fathers and Sons

One of the most impactful moments of the service was when J.D.'s boys took turns reading entries from their dad's daily log. Not surprisingly, virtually all the entries focused on his faith.

Jackson read the entry from June 6, 2003: "How do we stay unaffected by riches and honor God? Lord, may we be in your purpose, not get lazy and seduced by the world. Where man's treasure is, that's where his heart is also."

Miller read from March 21, 2004: "Lord, help me realize part of the reason I am here as president is to give back as much as I can. To whom much is given, much is required." And on July 5, 2012, J.D. wrote, "The greatest need of my family is my personal holiness."

Jason read the entry from September 9, 2004, where J.D. prayed, "I love hearing a song on the radio that reminds me how much God loves me or reading a story that causes my heart to glimpse the big picture that tells me that I matter in this battle."

And finally, Taylor read the entry from April 29, 2004, where J.D. prophetically wrote, "I know to count it all joy as I go through the wilderness.

I will be stronger for the Lord and His purposes because of it."

He poured his faith into those boys every day of their lives, and in the end, he reaped the rewards of that, both in the influence they are having on others and in the way they took care of him during those last five years.

When J.D.'s best friend, Dave Alpern, spoke at the service, he told those boys, "Your dad's nickname was 'son of.' Today we pass the title of 'son of' to you. Consider it a great honor to be considered the son of J.D. Gibbs." I can assure you, they do. And every time they reach out to someone else in need or share the gospel with someone, J.D. will reap the rewards of that as well.

A Friend in Need . . .

Remember when the devil told God that the reason Job loved Him was because of God's blessings and that if God took those things away, Job would turn on Him? After the devil *did* take everything away from Job, Job still loved the Lord. Well, I saw something similar play out between J.D. and his two best friends, Dave and Moose.

They all met as teenagers back when J.D. used to have everyone over to the house for Young Life gatherings. In fact, J.D. led both Dave and Moose to Christ. Anyway, they developed a close bond that extended well into adulthood. Their families would hang out together, and the guys would go on ski trips together every winter. They'd go to football games, baseball games, races—you name it. They just had a blast together. Then J.D. got sick. And I'm telling you, the way those guys rallied around him was amazing.

Of course, Dave saw J.D. every day at the office, and he and his wife would have J.D., Melissa, and the boys over for dinner as often as possible. And even though Moose lived out of state, he and Gumby—another of J.D.'s high school buddies— would come out once a month to visit J.D. and take the boys out for a nice evening. But what really struck me was that these guys continued to take ski trips together even after J.D. reached a point where he had to be monitored very closely. They didn't care. To them, J.D. was still J.D., and they were going to hit the slopes together just like they always had.

Then, when it got to the point where J.D. was unable to get around on his own anymore, his friends would come to the house, sit with J.D., and just rub his feet. Now Moose, in particular, was always a big, loud, larger-than-life character. I remember back when J.D. and his friends were teens, Pat and I would be lying in bed at eleven o'clock at night trying to sleep, and Moose would be over at the house for a Young Life party, rooting through the fridge and making all kinds of noise. Eventually I'd just yell out, "Moose, shut up already!" Well, to see him crouching quietly at the end of the sofa gently massaging J.D.'s feet during those final few months was a beautiful thing and a true testament to the friendship those boys shared. J.D. poured into them their whole lives, and when he needed them, they were there caring for him, even when he was unable to move, speak, or give them anything in return.

Dave has since stepped into J.D.'s old role as president of JGR, and both he and Moose spoke at J.D.'s memorial service. To this day, they continue to invest in J.D.'s boys, and I believe they always will. If that isn't reaping what you sow, I don't know what is.

Paying It Forward

The more I think about it, the more I believe my pastor friend, who I mentioned in chapter 3, was right. Our vision is limited to what is right in front of us. But God sees the bigger picture. He knows how the story ends. More important, He knows that our story doesn't end when we die. It just keeps going.

I've often said that in the end, all we have are the relationships we've made and the impact we've had on people. That's our legacy. Those are the seeds we sow. We build into others' lives. We help and support one another. We're there for one another in the good times and the bad. As Paul writes in 1 Thessalonians 5:11, "Encourage one another and build each other up."

J.D. *loved* people. Those were the seeds he sowed. And when the time came, the relationships he had built and the impact he had on others was his reward. The really amazing thing, though, is that even though J.D. is no longer with us, his impact is still going strong. I've already told you how important Young Life was to J.D. growing up. Well, one of his dreams was to start up a Young Life chapter in the underserved inner city areas of Charlotte. I've also told you that after J.D.'s service, we established a website, jdgibbslegacy.com, where people could go to learn more about his walk with the Lord. In addition to posting the complete memorial service, we also created a button where people could donate to an endowment fund to establish an inner city chapter of Young Life in J.D.'s name. As of this writing, $1.5 million has been donated, and J.D.'s dream has become a reality, meaning he will continue to play a role in leading others to Christ for many years to come.

So, did J.D. reap what he sowed? Yes, I believe he did. It was hard for me to see it when he was sick and even when he went to be with the Lord. But now, as I sit back and reflect on all the ways his life has impacted and continues to impact others, I can.

When Melissa was putting together J.D.'s obituary, she quoted John 12:24: "Very truly I tell you, unless a kernel of wheat falls to the ground and dies, it remains only a single seed. But if it dies, it produces many seeds."

As great as J.D.'s impact was in life, in death, it was far greater.

7
NEXT STEPS

IT HAPPENS EVERY SUNDAY. A quarterback throws the ball into heavy coverage and either gets picked or the pass gets batted away, and all the while, there was a guy wide open downfield. Why didn't he just throw it to that guy? Simple. He didn't see him. The commentators up in the booth love it when that happens, because they all look like geniuses for seeing what the quarterback couldn't. But they've got a bird's-eye view *and* instant replay.

When you go back over the video after the game, you see all the "coulda, shoulda" moments. Sitting there in the quarterback's room with a half-dozen camera angles at your disposal, everything is crystal clear. But when you're in the middle of a play, scrambling around in real time with a 285-pound defensive end coming straight at you, you can't always see things clearly.

That's kind of how I was operating for most of J.D.'s illness. I was so busy trying to figure out a way to help him, I couldn't see the bigger picture. But God saw all of it—every angle and every impact—right from the very beginning. He always does.

It's All about Perspective

When I share my testimony with people, I often compare life to a game of football, where we are the players, God is our head coach, and the Bible is our playbook. We've touched on a lot of that already. But there's one other piece I always bring up—the clock. No matter what's happening on the field, at some point, that clock is going to read 00:00. That's it. Game over.

Now, typically, the point I'm trying to make is that in the game of life, we don't know how much time we have left, which is why it's so important to make the decision to surrender our lives to Christ before our clock hits 00:00. I still believe that.

But one of the things I've learned since J.D. went home is that our clock and God's clock are different. We tend to look at things from an earthly perspective, but God looks at them from an eternal perspective. Here's what I mean by that.

I really struggled with the fact that I only got to spend forty-nine years with J.D. I wanted more time with him—here and now. But now I realize that those forty-nine years I had with J.D. on earth are only a drop in the bucket compared to the eternity I'm going to spend with him in heaven.

Likewise, J.D. may have suffered for five years here on earth, but now he is in the presence of his heavenly Father in perfect health, and he is going to be that way forever.

I can lament that I lost a wonderful son too early, or I can choose to celebrate that J.D.'s passing, while devastating to those of us who knew him well, has resulted in thousands of lives won for Christ. And I believe this is only the beginning.

My point is, God's vision is so much bigger than ours, and J.D.'s battle drove that point home for me in ways I'd never considered before.

The Big 5

When I walked off that stage at Belk Arena, I couldn't understand why God failed to show up during J.D.'s illness. I couldn't understand why J.D. had to suffer at all, let alone as much and as long as he did. I questioned whether there was a reason for J.D.'s suffering, and I questioned whether J.D. truly reaped the rewards of a life well lived. Once again, it came down to a question of perspective.

In my mind, for God to show up meant J.D.'s healing, and because I was so focused on that, I didn't see all the amazing ways and places that God *did* show up—at the Daytona 500, at that little restaurant, that day on the bleachers, and in all the friends, neighbors, doctors, and caregivers who rallied around J.D., Melissa, and their four boys. My point is, God may not always show up the way we want Him to, but that doesn't mean He isn't there. He is *always* there. He is there in the people who comfort us when we are hurting, who give us a shoulder to cry on when we are sad, and who reach out to us when we need help. Though there were days God felt very far away, the truth is, He has never been closer than He was during those five difficult years.

Not only was He there, He knew what was going to happen—even before J.D. showed the first signs of sickness. When someone we love is suddenly taken from us or falls gravely ill, it can sometimes feel like God is either powerless to stop it, or worse, that He is somehow responsible for it. But nothing could be further from the truth. God is all-knowing and all-seeing, and He loves us more than we can possibly comprehend. He doesn't send evil our way—it's just part of the package that comes from living in a fallen world. He never wanted or intended for us to experience sickness, pain, or death. We brought that on ourselves. But He does have a plan for us. And He only allows pain and suffering to enter our lives if it's going to wind up being the best for us in the end.

In J.D.'s case, God knew his suffering would produce a great testimony and that many would be led to Christ as a result. At first blush, that might not seem fair. I know it didn't to me. But part of living in a fallen world means taking the good with the bad. Yes, there will be pain and suffering. We will experience tragedy and loss.

But God also promises us that great glory awaits us on the other side. You can't have one without the other. But because God loves us, the good outweighs the bad astronomically. A friend of mine pointed out that the theme of the New Testament book 1 Peter is "Christlike suffering always brings Christlike glory." And that's a lesson I've come to see through J.D.

And while at first glance, J.D.'s loss didn't seem to measure up with the way he lived his life, I now realize that what J.D. received was far greater than what he lost. Death may seem like the end, but for followers of Christ, it is only the beginning. And just as I believe the full impact of J.D.'s life has yet to be seen, I also believe the full impact of our own lives won't fully be known to us until we are in heaven.

I didn't have clarity on this when J.D. went to be with the Lord, but now I do. And knowing that God loves us, that He has a plan for our lives, that there is meaning and value in our suffering, and that everything does work out for the best for those who love and serve the Lord has given me great peace after suffering what I can consider to be life's greatest heartbreak.

I also found peace in something Melissa said
at J.D.'s memorial service. Here's what she said:

> [J.D.] believed that God is real, the Bible
> is true, and that Jesus is worth emulating.
> While never doing it perfectly, he lived
> his life seeking to please God. It was a
> conscious choice, a daily, deliberate
> discipline, an intentional mindset. Not
> only did he think it was right; more
> important, he thought it was true. And
> when something of such importance is
> true, what else can you do but build your
> life on it and go all-in? That's what you
> saw—an authentic display of love and
> trust in the Creator of the universe and
> the Author of his personal story. That
> Creator and Author could have rewritten
> this ending. He didn't. And we don't
> have to understand why. Even when
> God doesn't do what we think is best, it
> doesn't change what's true. As much
> as it hurts that J.D. wasn't healed, he'd
> not want anyone to be disillusioned in
> the wake of his suffering. . . . Either it's
> true or isn't, and if it's true, we embrace

GAME PLAN FOR LOSS

all of it—even the parts we don't understand, even the parts that tempt us to turn away. . . .

One of my favorite Bible verses about heaven is 1 Corinthians 13:12, which reads, "For now we see through a glass dimly, but then face to face. Now I know in part, but then, I shall know fully, even as I am fully known." J.D. sees clearly now. He understands why all of this had to be. He is whole. He is at peace. He sees the face of Jesus, and he's full of joy.

An Invitation

Now, you may be thinking, *This is all well and good for you, Coach, but my loved one wasn't sold out for the Lord like J.D. was. He wasn't even a Christian. How does what you've said here apply to me?*

Listen, I get it. J.D. was an extraordinary young man. And I realize that because his last name was Gibbs, he was afforded some unique opportunities (like a car running in the Daytona 500 with his name on it). But here's the thing. I went to the Bible for answers to my questions because I didn't want someone's *opinion* about why my son suffered the way he did; I wanted the *truth*. That's what the Bible is—God's truth. It's *His* game plan for us. It tells us how we are supposed to live and act and treat one another.

Those verses I shared with you aren't just feel-good phrases pulled from some self-help book I picked up on Amazon. They are the inspired words of God—our Father and the Creator of the Universe. And they apply to all of us.

When God sent His one and only Son to suffer and die on the cross, He did that for all of us. He did it to undo what Adam and Eve did back in the Garden. He did it to give us a way back into Paradise and an opportunity to inherit eternal glory. God gave us an amazing gift. Whether we choose to accept it is entirely up to us.

My point is, God's promises don't just apply to guys like J.D. They apply to everyone who chooses to accept His gift of eternal life.

And if you are thinking, *My loved one didn't have an eternal impact on anyone*, stop for a second and think about why you're reading this book. Odds are, you picked this book up because you lost someone. And no matter what that person's circumstances were, their loss left you with questions—maybe some of the same questions

I had. I guess what I'm trying to say is, what if this book is God's way of showing up? Because believe me when I say, He does love you. He does have a plan for your life. And even though things might be difficult right now, He does want what is best for you.

If you are interested in taking that next step and responding to God, I would encourage you to start by saying this prayer:

> Lord, You know that I'm a sinner, and I know You sent your Son, Jesus Christ, to this earth. He lived a perfect life. And You allowed Him to go to the cross and be crucified for my sins. I ask You to come into my life, forgive me of my sins, and be my Lord and personal Savior.

If you sincerely acknowledge Jesus as your Lord, you will be on God's team—the one team that is guaranteed victory.

I would also encourage you to spend some time in God's Word. Start at the beginning or go right to the verses I've mentioned and read the rest of the story. Or better yet, start with the first book in the New Testament, Matthew. That's

Jesus' story. And it's ours, too. Remember, the Bible isn't just a book. It's God's game plan for us. If you don't have one, go to GamePlanForLife. com, click on "Get a Free Bible," and I'll send you one! Finally, I would encourage you to visit jdgibbslegacy.com and watch the memorial service. That will tell you everything you need to know.

When I lost J.D., I did not have a game plan for dealing with the grief and the heartache that followed. Now I do. I hope what I've shared has better prepared you to face the difficult days ahead. I hope you'll take God's words to heart. And I hope you'll consider taking that next step. I'll be praying for you.

Coach Gibbs

J.D. Gibbs
(photo courtesy of the Gibbs family archives, 2010)

J.D. and Coach, working the family business
(photo courtesy of JGR archives, 2004)

J.D., Melissa, Jackson, Miller, Jason, and Taylor
(photo by Sharon Clark, 2008)

JOE GIBBS has earned positions in the Pro Football Hall of Fame and the NASCAR Hall of Fame, having achieved a remarkable level of success in both professional sports. Gibbs served as head coach of the Washington Redskins from 1981 to 1992 and again from 2004 to 2007, leading the team to ten playoff appearances, four NFC Championship titles, and three Super Bowl Championships. He was also named to the NFL 100 All-Time Team in 2019 as one of the ten best football coaches in history. Amazingly, Gibbs has found comparable success in NASCAR, helping to lead Joe Gibbs Racing to five NASCAR Cup Series titles since it started racing in 1992. Gibbs started JGR with his older son, J.D., who passed away in January of 2019 following a long battle with a degenerative neurological disease. His legacy continues through the J.D. Gibbs Legacy Fund's support of the Young Life ministry, as well as through the sharing of his story, which can be found at jdgibbslegacy.com. Gibbs's younger son, Coy, is now leading the family's NASCAR operations as chief operating officer. Joe and his wife, Pat, live in North Carolina near their eight grandchildren.

NOTES

CHAPTER 2: "WHY DIDN'T GOD SHOW UP?"

1. This story is adapted from chapter 10 of my book *Game Plan for Life: Your Personal Playbook for Success* (Carol Stream, IL: Tyndale, 2011).

CHAPTER 3: "ARE WE JUST LIVING A LIFE OF CHANCE?"

1. What follows is adapted from chapters 1 and 3 of my book *Game Plan for Life: Your Personal Playbook for Success* (Carol Stream, IL: Tyndale, 2011).

CHAPTER 5: "WHY DO SOME CHRISTIANS SUFFER MORE THAN OTHERS?"

1. C. S. Lewis, *The Problem of Pain* (New York: HarperCollins, 2001), 91.

The North Carolina Field Minister Program

The field minister candidates are incarcerated men serving fifteen years to life. These men earn a four-year bachelor of arts degree in pastoral ministry with a secondary emphasis on counseling. Upon graduation they will be deployed to prisons throughout the state of North Carolina to serve as counselors and chaplains.

Key goals of this program:
- higher education in prison
- giving lifers a purpose
- training the incarcerated to be chaplains
- making a difference from the "inside out"
- reduction in recidivism
- spiritual transformation to moral rehabilitation
- lead many to a personal relationship with the Lord

The NCFMP is a partnership with Game Plan for Life, the Department of Public Safety, and Southeastern Baptist Theological Seminary. Founded by Coach Joe Gibbs in 2016. For more information or to donate please visit gameplanforlife.com

Game Plan for Life is a 501(c)(3) non-profit incorporated in 2016.

"I have fought the good **fight**,
I have **finish**ed the race,
and I have **remain**ed **faithful**."

2 Timothy 4:7, NLT

To learn more about JD Gibbs' legacy, please visit
jdgibbslegacy.com